FROZEN LATITUDES

Frozen Latitudes

Poems

Therése Halscheid

Press 53
Winston-Salem

Press 53, LLC
PO Box 30314
Winston-Salem, NC 27130

First Edition

A TOM LOMBARDO POETRY SELECTION

Cover design by Kevin Morgan Watson

Cover art, "I Will Endure This Solitary," Copyright © 2014
by David Hayward, used by permission of the artist.

Author photo by Doreen Totaro Fera

Printed on acid-free paper
ISBN 978-1-941209-12-7

for Charles, my father

Acknowledgments

The author is grateful to editors of the following magazines in which these poems appeared in original or previous forms, and to *Pudding House Publications* for a chapbook award *Greatest Hits*. A special thanks to journals for contest awards: *Comstock Review* for "Trash Day" Third Place; *Exit 13* for "My Father's Cereal" Third Place; *New Millennium Writings* for "Lost Sense of Self" Honorable Mention; *Tiferet* for "The Rooms" First Place and "Certain Shadows Over the Mountain" a Finalist Award.

The Barnwood International Poetry Mag: "Letter of Stones" formerly titled "Reading the Stones"
Bellevue Literary Review: "Visiting Dementia"
Best Poem: "Harpooning the Whale"
Blueline: "The Asking," "Reading the Thoughts of Clouds"
California Quarterly: "Turns"
Cold Mountain Review: "Phrases Strong and Perfect"
Comstock Review: "Trash Day," "Wordless"
Connecticut Review: "After Alaska"
Crab Orchard Review: "The Bottom Stones"
Exit 13: "My Father's Cereal"
Fidelities (South Africa): "Dreamscape" "The Air Child, I."
Ginosko (England): "Aerial View"
Identity Theory: "The Walk Home"
Imagination and Place–Weather: "The Telling Wind"
Jerseyworks: "Morning Prayer for Pink," "Geriatric Chair," "Visiting Dementia"
Mid-America Poetry Review: "The Naming"
Mochila Review: "Currents"
Naugatuck River Review: "Making the Eskimo Clothes"
Paterson Literary Review: "When Just Enough Words Have Gathered At Windows," "The Death of Your Body," "Wooden Rosary"
Philadelphia Stories: "The Air Child, II."
Public-Republic: (Bulgaria) "The Asking," "Internal World"
Schuylkill Valley Journal: "River River," "The Open Book"
Sulphur River Literary Review: "Air in the Room," "Geriatric Chair"
Tattoo Highway: "The Yukon Quest"
Thatchwork: "Rowing the Sky"
Tiferet: "Enlightenment," "Harpooning the Whale," "The Rooms," "Certain Shadows over the Mountain"

Wordgathering. A Journal of Disability Poetry and Literature: "Unsoundness of Mind"

Up and Under QND Review: "Hometown"

US 1 Worksheets: "Land of No Time," "Making A Path Called *Charles*," "Mother,"

Frozen Latitudes

Introduction by Tom Lombardo   xi

I

When Just Enough Words Have Gathered at Windows...   3
Trash Day   4
Phrases Strong and Perfect   5
Lost Sense of Self   6
My Father's Cereal   7
River River   8
Clan of the Owl   9
Currents   10
Rowing the Sky   11
Omen: 4:00 am   12
Mother   13
Land of No Time   14
Heart Bright   15
Internal World   16
The Air Child, I.   17
The Yukon Quest   19
The Air Child, II.   21
The Walk Home   23
Unsoundness of Mind   25
After Alaska   26
Wooden Rosary   27
Morning Prayer for Pink   28
Enlightenment   29

II

Hometown   33
Wordless   34
Air in the Room   35
The Telling Wind   36
Geriatric Chair   37

The Naming   38
Hard Reply of a Hand   39
Letter of Stones   40
The Open Book   42
The Rooms   43
The Channeler   44
The Asking   45
Making the Eskimo Clothes   46
White Sock   47
Visiting Dementia   48
Dreamscape   49
Harpooning the Whale   50
The Death of Your Body   52
Turns   53
Mother,   54
The Bottom Stones   55
Making a Path Called *Charles*   56
Aerial View   58
Reading the Thoughts of Clouds   61
Certain Shadows Over the Mountain   62
The Cleansing   64
When Just Enough Words...   66

Introduction
by Tom Lombardo
Press 53 Poetry Series Editor

In this incredibly cold and warm collection, poet Therése Halscheid melds two journeys into a metaphoric chronicle of daily struggles against impossible odds where lives are at the very edge of survival. Ms. Halscheid's *Frozen Latitudes* is rooted in two specific latitudes. One is a literal location in the far northern Arctic land where she lived among the clans of the White Mountain Inupiaq tribe.

Through the oral tales she heard from elders and her own observations, Ms. Halscheid unveils the native people's dependence upon ice, water, hunting, and fishing in a land where a father, while sitting inside his tent, learns of his son's death and

> a white owl rose
>
> out of nowhere continuing through
> the top of the tent into the sky.
>
> ...it was like the spirit of his son
> was in the form of an animal and there
>
> was a strange light around and wind like
> a slight brushing of feathers and feathers as
>
> the sound of death passing through to
> the other side of the world.
>
> [from "Clan of the Owl"]

This is a mystical place where "even the wind blows as God's breath."

The second location of *Frozen Latitudes* also depends on God's breath, but is much closer to home. It's the place and time where her father's life was frozen, when during heart surgery

an error occurred on the operating table
when...my father lacked oxygen
long enough to erase from his memory
the years he had with us:

days with us, hours of our good life with him
gone, his mind without Time.

[from "Mother"]

The poet was fourteen years old when her father exited
surgery aphasic and demented. He lived thirty years while she
and her mother cared for him, their own lives moving
uncertainly forward in time. He was trapped in "the land of no
time," just as The Real People in the northern interior of Alaska,
where

the present is one continuing moment—
the body moves to natural rhythms, is fluid with seasons
living the way a river does...

and where

there is no passage of time, only change
in the coming and going of moon, in the wind that blows freely
from the cold outer edge
of the world.

[from "Land of No Time"]

Frozen Latitudes is a collection where bottom stones of an
Alaskan river—which The Real People call "oracles from the
sea"—are as telling as lotus in a muddy riverbed in Maine. It is
a collection where the link between Yupik hunters and the mind
of a whale, which presents itself sacrificially, becomes the
connection the poet imagines in her father's voice

easing
into a clarity
I had not known
in thirty years

...I flew alert
toward weatherless light

...a forgiving
breeze which knows

...what I only wanted
to be
your good father.

[from "Aerial View"]

Ms. Halscheid weaves two threads together skillfully in a type of poetic magical realism. Her poems reached into the winter of my soul, freezing and thawing my emotions as I read.

I

When Just Enough Words Have Gathered at Windows...

as breath becomes patterned there
        as icy flakes

        after all
           has been
              said

repeated to
only
myself   alone
                in a room

    is

      stuck
to panes whitened
      like cold swollen lakes—

     when all of it's

over
suddenly   onto the glass

     like tiny crystals

        I want to break through,
          mouth open
voice
carried across

      everything
      opaque

sentence after sentence moving   words
   over the winter earth,

     my father out of me.

Trash Day

This is how it really looked long ago....

This is myself back in time, a girl
with sallow skin, dragging metal cans to the curb,
notice how I stand for awhile that far from our house
watch how my lips, bright as scars, are parting
open with words so the great air can take them
out of their mystery—

see how my thoughts form the storms, how the morning sky
fills with dark sentences

always something about aphasia, his dementia,
something always about my father caught
so quiet inside me

that would rise in the wind to become
something readable.

I am only fourteen. But you can tell I look old
as if life is ending. Notice how my limbs droop so
willow-like over the trash, see how the cans
are all packed with food, know I am starving myself, I am
that full of my father....

These are our neighbors, each turning in their sleep as they wake,
each waking as they turn from their room to the window
watching the weather above them.

And this is an image of the whole town in shock.
See how they dread my gray hovering grief, just watch
as they walk, how they carry on with the endless clouds
I made weekly, correctly, so very awful and coming
into their eyes.

Phrases Strong and Perfect

Inupiaq tribe—White Mountain, Alaska

To the Eskimo, glances are actions. And of actions,
they leave a bright trail to read

so that when two crows hit against the glass window
where Linky was, she said, *something has happened!*

She said nothing comes here without significance, that
even the wind blows as God's breath

shaking the willows, taking its leaves. She said
what I said, that even dusk talks in long sentences of color;

everything that shifts, moves, but not only for itself
like the sun dropping a strong phrase of light

on a child, like the child giving a crow call
the same moment Linky sights the birds.

This is what the cold has taught. How the world is
of words though no one is speaking

how the days went as this day went,
which has nothing to do with time.

Lost Sense of Self

Yesterday my father greeted me
from another time—

I was his sister,
and the day before that I was his wife,
tomorrow I might be his mother
or Aunt Mamie

and then, of course, there are moments
within these off-moments
when I am mistaken for someone
no longer alive, a person
he once knew

or perhaps I am only
a stranger in passing—

and why I am telling you so,
is to share how
the longing to be myself
has come to mean being alone

which is to say of these days that
I am now starving myself
in the attic.

Fourteen, too frail of a girl—
too hard to take the body
into these hours,
where the world continues with
no thoughts of me

where I continue to be anything but
a child of his.

My Father's Cereal

We wake on dry land where the sun works brilliant—

until a bib is tied about my father's neck
a bowl is placed high upon books

and the largest spoon in the house is set in his hand
between two crooked fingers.

There is my mother creating this daily scene of events
pouring Cheerios into his bowl

adding the white milk before guiding
my father's spoon down into it.

She leaves the room then and there is only myself
sitting across from him.

I have my own bowl but do nothing about it.

We are a pair, of sorts. I refuse how his face is unreadable
that his brain is damaged enough to believe he is eating

and he is blind to the point where he thinks I look fine.

When we move, we move as slow water moves
barely along because nothing can save us.

His spoon floats through air, is empty, is treading in space,
my thoughts are all garbled as if made of liquid....

We remain this way, my father and I
as if under water

the Cheerios turn soggy, inflating like inner tubes
but it is too late—

soon we will drown in this moment

day will begin, and there will only be the strange surfacing
of our tragic lives.

River River

we are going into its untamed center
into a flow that never finishes
until we become like the clouds
the river takes to its surface,
and the mirrored trees,
the shadows suddenly stretched,
until the whole story of ourselves
is upside-down and we turn
unrecognizable in its gesture
denying the power of
waves until they are on us, until
we are in them.

Clan of the Owl

tale of an Inupiaq tribe

When Alan drowned, Rose said his father knew
yet no one told him.

Percy was up river when his son's snowmobile broke
through the ice. At that moment

the sun came and the wild place brightened.
Percy was the only one there

to see how the day arrived
with its story of death.

Rose added that
Percy had stayed at the fish camp too long

right at the river's mouth where
he always pitched but this time he was caught

as it was November, meaning
Fish River turned soggy, it's

soft spots were deceiving,
it would freeze at night and melt during the day.

Alan was in a snowmobile going small under the ice,
his eyes frozen open, his mouth locked in his very last word.

Percy was in his tent, just sitting when
the canvas became illuminated, and a white owl rose

out of nowhere continuing through
the top of the tent into the sky.

The way Rose tells it was like the spirit of his son
was in the form of an animal and there

was a strange light around and wind like
a slight brushing of feathers and feathers as

the sound of death passing through to
the other side of the world.

Currents

The idea of a river suffering
from its reflection

is what might happen
should you ever see well enough

to notice yourself, or be given
new eyes

or the mindflow
to use any breeze

that would force
your mirrored image into action

up out of its murkiness

the damaged
brain, and then

watch how your limbs might take on
a certain kind of fluidity

begin waving me
near you again

calling me daughter—

while I cry like high tide
as you continue speaking

in the slow manner
of ancient waters

that I would want
to wade

to the voice
father, into your rippling arms.

Rowing the Sky

before surgery, his deceased mother appeared to him in a dream

I had long left earth
when I returned in a dream,
and you slept while I came with love in my eyes
and you dreamt of my wearing that look
while braving the sea.

There was a sound to my oars,
a steady cutting noise

risky pieces of fog
and beyond a letter floating,
something heaven-sent
which surfaced upon the foretelling waters

something drifting
for me to avert your tragic fate—

it was there,
played out in waves
coming, coming as it has always been
the way of prophesy, to act out
an awful knowing....

Son, when the boat stilled,
even as waves paused,
why did you not trust
that night
was an honest realm of wind
where I could warn softly, sadly—

yes, night broke into words
as I read what I knew
before paddling backwards, into the stars.

Omen: 4:00 a.m.

When, in the early hours
before your open-heart surgery,

the sky began talking, each twinkle a word
each word a language of light,

I learned that
speaking in tongues meant

even inanimate objects could
transfer a message.

There was the moon and its voice.
The star, the dread of its speech.

My face at the screen kept
pressed to the attic bedroom window.

My father, I say to you now
whatever light my own body held

I gave back to the night,
as if it could soar like a warning,

a white sentence, quite readable,
to force you away from your hospital bed.

Mother

had one too. A premonition.
After the prayer she made
the morning of her husband's surgery,
sun squinting through stained glass
casting rainbows across
the church's floor.

I caught how her hands were
to her lips: upright, clasped as a quivering steeple.
I slightly heard her prayer blown
through them by the holy wind
of her breath.

And of course I was there
in the waiting room when a knowing took place
that the strength she asked for would be given,
was coming as she had sent for it
only now she knew exactly
what this meant.

I don't remember her hands in that instant
of her knowing, but know her well enough
to suggest they fell limp to her lap;
that her eyes grew large from
what her lips knew but
could not yet say.

And I have always thought
her revelation happened the same moment
an error occurred on the operating table,
when her husband, my father, lacked oxygen
long enough to erase from his memory
the years he had with us:

days with us, hours of our good life with him
gone, his mind without Time.

Land of No Time

the northern interior, Alaska

In a place of always light or always dark, in the arctic north,
there are no required hours, no hurry for the future
and little thought of the past

the present is one continuing moment—
the body moves to natural rhythms, is fluid with seasons,
living the way a river does

how it carries what comes to it
returns to land, what it was tossed

or think of it this way, choosing when to wake, when to sleep
think of the summer when the sun is constant
all during the summer, when day ends
the light does not

and it is like that
living without the clock

you cannot schedule this part of the earth
there is no passage of time, only change
in the coming and going of moon, in the wind that blows freely
from the cold outer edge
of the world.

Heart Bright

the heart's view

Charles, too many years
you have continued
as I do

unseen
and easily ignored

long forgotten by surgeons

who entered
the hours
where time did not pass

and took under
their sudden lights

my aching
form, to be held
in their plump hands
and broken
until they at last scrubbed
their minds of it.

Troublemaker!
they said of me then.

I heard them.

Yet I was where
all your compassion
and soft pity
moved and I was

where love always
was running—

the brightest flow
of red
before you became
vacant-eyed.

Internal World

father's view

Do not force me to want these
shadowy doctors
and faint strangers
or look anymore
at their leaning over

not when I can open my eyes inward,
not while I watch, as in sleep,
memories inside me:
forgotten films, old reels
of my life replaying.

Look, here is my wife
and me, with our daughter—
we are in the Volkswagen
riding along some imagined highway.

It's blossom time,
cherry petals all off the trees
see through the car's window
our hair blown by the repetitive wind,
which is actually the air
from my breath, the very inhale
that keeps this image alive,
the drive going....

The Air Child
I.

During the first
autumn of not eating

there was still
air in me, and water, and hidden letters.

There was the forged path
through the forest
where I kept walking
to school

tossing the sandwich
my mother made daily,
against the base of the tree
that I loved

and then shivered
in sagging skin

against its strong bark, leaned
for a time
before moving on.

There was
the tree which I loved
that would weep at the very center
of itself

whenever a letter would rise
from my throat

and the open air
would read
that something was wrong, so wrong

said the loud wind
to the woods

until the shuddering
green leaves would begin
their own draining
of strength, of color, becoming

insipid, the same
as me.

The Yukon Quest

for Greg Parvin

What was it like when the sled spun on a river
frozen enough to create a deceptive sheen,

that moment, when his body lifted in wind, sled and all,
while the huskies were held in mid-air

before falling to the watery surface
only to wipe out once more on the overflow.

What was it like after the whirling ended, when his body quieted,
the pack too, when the world came back to their eyes

and they saw land again as it first seemed, everything the same,
such vast areas of white

they sped in the wrong direction. With snow blown
over the musher's tracks they lost their way

and could do nothing, had lost their way
braving the barrenness.

Imagine the shock at sighting their previous camp,
and the sharp turns he made to set off once more

just as the moon rose over the mountains, racing once more,
riding the long road, the smooth long road of the moon;

of his growing concern when food ran out for the pack
when the dogs refused to go on

and bedded down in small nests of snow and lay there and there
were fierce winds, the lost feeling in his fingers.

Imagine his eyes smarting as the sun fully returned
when he trudged to a distant tree

broke a few branches only to find them green—
and the hours which followed when his sweat froze

and he thought of the dogs surrounded by stillness
everything whitened as with mists in a dream.

Think of the power needed to deny his own urge to sleep,
and stay obedient to his course walking the hills for dry wood

until an abandoned miner's camp came into view,
where he stacked some wood in his arms

before starting back to the dogs, knowing he would lose the race
but had just won something far more important.

Picture then, after crossing his own finish line,
when he began a fire, poked a branch in a drift to hang his clothes to dry

that he stood before the great flickering flame, bare-chested in forty below
with nothing around for miles, only the dogs and himself.

There, he quietly raised his hands in thanks
knowing it was enough to watch

how the moon moved slowly over them
the old moon, so silvery, that round and silvery moon in the arctic sky.

The Air Child
II.

Into the second season
of not eating

there was still Time in me, enough
stored hours to keep trekking
to school,

always taking
the path through the forest,
through frost

and white air which held
the woods and me captive....

You could see it in the way
we began suffering alike, wearing
the same look

of bare sorrow—

you could tell by the way
my legs were

thin as winter grasses,
steps so light that they left no tracks

and even in the way
the outer colors of earth drew inward
and down, the same as I

was withdrawing myself
from the world, as I was

removing myself
from my father.

This was nothing that clothes could hide—
this is what Death wanted

this leafless body, this girl

alone
and failing

against the cold trunks of trees,
the bones of them.

The Walk Home

Each day the curtains part from each home we pass
and without clearly seeing them
I can sense the widening eyes of mothers, I can feel
their thoughts through the windows
and it is all about the way
my father and I look
to them.

It is about it being late spring and the fact that
he and I wear woolen coats and gloves
as we are always cold, our lives so dark
not even the sun can
save us.

It is about my looking less than human, brittle-boned,
slumped, I am that thin—

and certainly, it is the sight of my father beside me
who is near blind and brain damaged,
someone behaving in ways that one might find
in mental wards.

Sometimes, their curtains are torn far apart
so fast as if fate landed an illusion, something
that never should be, and nothing appears real
except for their manicured lawns
and the distance the sidewalks allow
each afternoon, at 3:00, as we shuffle past this
place of groomed grass and the scent of
immediate flowers.

Above us are always the
overhanging trees whose blossoming
leaves spread glorious and are just like
a wedding arbor.

So perfect, I think, for this really is
what we are married to—

this aisle, this arm-in-arm walk
after school from my aunt's house to ours
this street like an obvious map of us,
pointing things out that
we cannot escape.

Unsoundness of Mind

Because I needed a father more than myself,
because I cherished my father,
I kept seeing things I could not say
I kept not saying until it became important
not to talk.

This was after the life he lived
had left his face.

This was each afternoon, after school,
when the rooms of our house took me in
through something loathsome

and there was my father
shape-shifting into monsters, he was there
with a horrid look, wearing fierce or faraway eyes.

I turned speechless about that
which could not be formed into sentences,
and perhaps certain behaviors should not be
given the power of expression

no words,
nothing to say of deranged hours

not a thing to do but pardon,
as we pardoned, always, making enough allowances
as to go on.

After Alaska

for Lisa

She lives in me now, in the north of my chest, where it is all dark, all winter—
to my ears will come her voice, then to my eyes, this white woman,
then pathways to the tribe she roamed with, to places inside me
where they are hunting and she is gathering and there, a certain arrow,
and there, a stab of certain pain

then to moments other than these, to nights when my heart is a drum
for her dancing and her movements tell stories, and I feel in her feet
all that was told to me, all that was shared.

When I breathe and the wind blows in a mighty power, my mouth forms
a small opening and she scales the dark throat to leap where
my lip catches the light, that she might sit
and be warmed for a while—

I felt her once, during an inner storm, as a certain chill ran through,
after my muscles tightened into big cold mountains
that she was arranging my ribs, arching them same as the shelters
she spoke of, in the icy north of Alaska, where they shape
whalebone over driftwood and pack it with sod.

There is a veined landscape she traverses in the spring
where my blood runs as thawed rivers

and she waits on the sands of myself for the return of the whale,
propped against a white embankment of bones, knees drawn to her chest
as in the way of the Eskimo, at times looking up, reading
the starry pores, the sky of my cloudless skin.

Wooden Rosary

I am strung sorrow, beaded secrets.

I contain agony
that never is spoken

all those vigilant mornings

of the same
pink sun

stepping through windows

illuminating
your strangeness
of the sun

entering the dark
time of your daughter
lost in that
long starvation—

swollen, I am
full of such stories

pinched tightly, prayed to

always
carried about

for is it not always about

how to go on
this hour and that hour

through thousands of dawns, decades

years of
your wife's sudden reaching

In the name of the Father ...

her hands
taking me to her

And of the Son ...

Morning Prayer for Pink

Messenger of morning, sign of the sun coming,
let it live on our bodies as well as the waking sky, let it be
the sudden blush, the shade of the tongue
which colors our speech

let it appear as the pale skin of the palm, any palm,
as with the luster of meadows, any meadow, say it has been so
since creation and will go on.

When we pause to listen, let us hear pink
as a musical note, the sound of it innocent,
first tone of the heart before it ripens
into red love. Let it be.

Let us touch it and say of pink it is neither salt, nor silk,
but the feeling of pleasure, smooth-skinned as petals, the bud
hidden between a woman's legs.

And when autumn ends and colors fade wearily from things,
let us see pink as a constant, long shade of dawn
and praise and praise pink and beyond that
say nothing more.

Do not claim it as being meant only for boy or for girl,
do not confine it, not when it is the first hue we wake to, not when
it crosses freely over the trees, down through
the crooks of them painting the ponds to look
like freshly squeezed grapefruit. Let it be.

And though the mind cannot see, let it sense
through our eyes how pink remains
like permanent dye, staining the soles of our feet, that part of us
stepping over the old earth, leading us through evening light
to where the sun moves down.

Enlightenment

Regarding the lotus,
they have their beginnings in dark places
at the very bottom of things, of lakes and of
shallow rivers, growing from the muck up, a frond
navigating itself, fronds

long and green, leaving the muddy riverbed
its rocky silences.

Think of the stem
when its murky secret becomes its body's truth,
think of the bud needing air
to open, needing to struggle without saying
and this is considered pure, this

is the white blossom
becoming light itself, on the surface of water.

II

Hometown

One fall

meant the end
of your being there—

Mother was away

and I could not foresee
what would occur

as you
at last rose
from the leather chair

yet saw
in that moment
of bone snapping inside you

how far I had entered
every extreme of your illness

to know
what brittleness lie
beneath your skin.

I could feel your hip break—

and could sense
how the walls of wind
worked
to betray you

and of time rushing
too quick
for my arms to rescue.

It was
as if

our house wanted you down Father,
in a tragic instant.

Wordless

moving into the Veterans Memorial Home

Dusk keeps dragging
its darkness
into the back garden
over the old stones
of the dead

I say nothing about it—

cannot talk without teeth or
the memory of words
that formed their sounds
through them

nor can I stay
in this quiet body

at night, mistaken for mist,
it will be me who moves
gossamer-like, out of myself,
beyond the ringlet of trees
and the soldiers' graves

toward scenes
that I dream of

once more placing
the name of
my wife on my tongue,
name of my daughter—

and in that place
imagine

what air
would again hold
if I could speak
where I am,
how I loved them.

Air in the Room

Too often is this
sudden lure

because your mouth has opened,
because your skin is lined
with begging pores

all of you
a dreaded entrance

that I
must go through
good-willed and giving,
lighting weak caves in your body.

But give me your words,
I whisper

that I might wear
what is unspoken outward

into the world
at large. *Breathe*

and learn how committed I am
to rush your cry towards
the screen window

through
the renewing blue

then fly recovering
against the farthest trees.

The Telling Wind

Wales, Alaska

If, in this moment I speak with a voice
it is to say of the ground, it is not fit for trees

nothing grows here but snow
the ice fog moves with nothing to cling to

if I am to speak of the land's lonely beauty
it is to say of both winter and summer, the color is white

it is to tell of the natural spring
set against the flank of a mountain

and how the people all come to it
going in sleighs with raw air freezing their lungs.

Of the salty sea, the vast Bering Sea,
to mention that even it freezes

which is to say where walrus are lounging on icebergs
and how, in late spring, the waves house the whale

and of the sky, a sky so shockingly cold, it is to add how
the moon appears with an open mouth.

If, as air, I speak—
if what I speak of is enough

to brush back the thin dry snow
it is to show you the graves of the dead

it is to say of the dead that
all the winters in them, their bodies remember.

Geriatric Chair

It is not ever over.

Always, each day,
wherever the quiet light hits
I am to faithfully hold you

take to my leather skin
what you have become—

the listlessness of the body

the way you are
no more remembering

and cannot see

the varied sun spots
on the floor
that we are
continually pushed to,
to warm all
your leaning hours.

Still no part of you moves

and I
can do nothing
but at last breathe
at night, with the lights out
alone.

The Naming

My body

continues the distance as if
without me.

It is Christmas Day.

It is any day
as they are all

returned
to this hesitancy—

the slow act
of nearing a solarium,
of cupping your sunlit shoulder.

My father,
how much risk this is

to witness
a room with your silence

to enter
without hope of language

and see through the absence,
in air

the timid flight of my hand

and how
your mouth only moves
to swallow back
words

even the small sound
which means me

gift that you gave—

present that I ask
and still listen for.

Hard Reply of a Hand

You can at least call me loyal.

Say I obey your dim, whispering mind —
what's left of it.

Admit that I honor its *Will*
to keep moving

trying, but not as we once did
all those fragrant mornings

plucking summer flowers for Mary,
your wife, while she lay sleeping.

How very much I loved
our life then, extending as we would

your arm leading me through
the truthful garden.

Now my only move is to leave
the sun's light on your lap

taking that arduous drive
to the furrowed brow above your eyes.

Your nurses have even gloved me
to stop this. Yet,

when they are not looking am I
finding ways of doing just as you want,

rubbing your head hard, the skin,
until it bleeds.

Letter of Stones

Bishops Beach—Homer, AK

I wrote of the beach half-frozen in middle March,
of walking its hardened surface, and the way of my walk,
the timeless strides crossing the snow-covered sands to Kachemak Bay.
I noted the bay's silvery current, the forming of small lips of water
and what they mouthed.

There is mention of the cobbles, so many cold and black,
shiny as patent leather. They were gleaming
because of the tide that rose and receded, it washed over
leaving a film that iced instantly in the Alaskan air.
There is a line that reads: *Above, the sun aimed at the beach*
but the thin sheet of the ice on the stones did not melt.
And it was so.

All this I wrote, of the curling of water, of the shapes of the cobbles,
but then added the look of them was beyond stones, more like *beings*
come ashore, gathered to talk with us as if they have something to say

and then went on to include another story of water
how, when spring thaws the sea, the first waves are for drinking
because the salt sinks and the top is fresh. This I learned in Alaska.
It was told to me and was true I could tell.

Think now what I understand.
Think of the pen moving hurriedly across the paper
because scenes rush to the page sometimes, too fast for the hand.

Later, further on, I explain how necessary it was
to be a little by myself, to stand in the shallows, cold by the water's edge.
I stood bundled in borrowed clothes, I wrote,
while the north wind I breathed
moved under my skin.

Of the stones they appear time and again, in one account
I pause over them staring as I would with meadow-flowers,
bent over so very low, yielding to something hard to explain.
Something the stones held within them, for I realized
learning was a bodily thing.

Toward the end I include an important story of The Real People,
which is the meaning of the word Eskimo, and how
they considered the stones as oracles from the sea.
They could read the strands of white granite running through
as lines of luck and erotic messages. They could turn a stone belly up
and something was known from a single touch.

I began touching the stones and talk of this:
Whatever is realized is right, I wrote, *and so we must touch
that our eyes, our hands will know what the stones have given of themselves,
the white lines like paths for us
to follow their rocky truths.*

The Open Book

How is it when you rarely know someone
that in one gesture, a story unfolds.

Like a week ago, sitting across from me,
your eyes had a whole page behind them.
And a few weeks before, your lips formed a chapter
without mouthing a word.

Today, when we parted, you took me to you
and your hands, the language of hands were suddenly readable.
Your fingers went from you like strewn sentences
to where my shoulder blades arched
like sides of an open book.

Love, I want to say, I want to say, *love*
touches the body, the entire body. Let it be

the room is an open tale, let us say the ceiling has stars:
wishful, burning, exploding to earth.

The Rooms

Mountain Light Sanctuary

A road led to the water that ribboned the mountain.
And not wanting to disturb a brook's rushing thoughts
I walked the rest of the way, softly
into other moments I wanted
to see and hear.

Beyond the rickety bridge and bamboo gate, the world
turned clear and the long distance to get there
was gone and ahead the green
land glistened.

Then, in the sunlight, in the sunlight, there—

were small rooms, open, of three sides only, each
facing the elements of ground and sky
each with a bed, candle or lamp, a bowl
for cool water but that
was all.

One room perched in the crook of a tree,
another just over the water, while others were set in hollows
or upon a bright spread of grass, as if
the old earth had made them,
this place.

How could it be otherwise; how could it not be—

that later, our own bodies would open
with stars entering, and night, and the wind.

The Channeler

Who can live in your kind of house—

the ruined walls of your body, sadness
that aches in the mess
of damaged cells.

My father, in dreaded ways I have entered
all the sick rooms in you, I have been
to the woman who breathed
a luminous being into herself
and spoke of your life

how your spirit looks forward to leaving—

how your soul has already detached
from the physical self
is half-risen out of you, hovering
above that look
of vacancy.

What is it then that holds you to earth?

Which prayer, what safe blessing
is needed to allow you to go
happily into clouds?

The Asking

I have just finished sweeping
a place in the glade where
a bed is now made of
star moss and blossoms.
I have ordered a moon
to come softly, its white
through the trees,
birds for the sky, a waterfall
lovely to listen to.

Come,

step out of the dream
of your house
onto the path of warm fog
in the scented opening
of the forest.
Follow the birds I have sent
and the light between leaves
where the pale of the moon
angles down through
the branches.

Listen. Be led
by only these things.
Nothing you leave will be missed.

Take no clothes,
you will not need them.

Making the Eskimo Clothes

1970s—Point Lay, Alaska

In the far far north, after your first hunt
I imagine your Inupiaq mother-in-law making a fire to warm you,
handing you a bone needle and sinew as thread.

You are in a place unreachable by roads.
You are newly wed and your face glows with the love you carry
and she is showing you how to sew
rather than speaking a language you do not yet understand.
And later that year, I imagine your understanding
but not needing to speak
for even the earth stretches wordlessly—
and isn't it so, the mouth is a circle of silence
whenever there's awe:

> *remember, the intestine of seal is stretched tissue thin*
> *before lining the mukluks*

> *remember, the wolverine hood is rimmed with claws*
> *to repel the snow ...*

You, in a small tribe of thirty; you hunting the white bear in winter
and in summer, eating the leaves off the trees.

Lisa, when you opened the barn door and light shone on the box
where these clothes were hidden
I asked to be taken to this place where ice never melts.
I found the coldest spot in the barn where the moment could take me.

Everything turned ice clear then and hunting,
you came over the wide windswept tundra,
over the starched snow, hunting.
Lisa, wearing your wide Eskimo coat lined with the fur of the bear
embroidered in bright colors, your tracks stitching the land.

White Sock

eventually a sock was placed on his hand to prevent his forehead from bleeding

They stitched your name
down the white length of me

and that meant
the end of walking,
that stopped the crunching sound
of the leaves, the touching green
of the grass.

C h a r l e s ...
it said simply.

But what it meant
really, was to endure
being worn
on your hand

and what that became for me
was to live my life lifting
to your forehead, running
without a landscape
of reason

rubbing your damaged brain,
to seek a sort of consciousness.

Visiting Dementia

                        The weeping
            at least
allows us someplace to be
            and your room is defined.

            It is what
      keeps us to each other

      the joining force—

for can you not feel what the sky
      has wanted

            its strong pull
                  at your drowsy will

                        tugging
            that draws
your expression up into it.

Lately, I have noticed rains
            Father, I have seen your eyes
            clouded over

            that look of yours
                  busy elsewhere

spotting angels.

                  When at last
            they fully enter this air
            for you

I will have almost nothing afterward—

      I will lose that long term
                  of belonging

                  to illness.

Dreamscape

The night shows
nothing more of you moves

yet even in dreams
you are managing the impossible
long air through your body, breathing
and no one knows what to do
not the nurse nor anyone else
that I see

in sleep
see that look of you

gasping for air
like a fish out of water,
your lips puckered where you are
not giving up
your mouth to the sky.

What is it about here
that grounds you so much to this
planet, that has me reliving
the same emergency
in dreams, as in life?

There is no waking
to anything different.

Harpooning the Whale

He came to the poetry reading
in the town library in Homer

a tall burly man with long hair and a beard,
wearing a necklace of bear claws and a polar bear tooth

a thousand years old, an amulet
an Eskimo medicine man had given him.

He roamed the bush for twenty years, he said,
and I am always on the move, I said,

and we had the same look in us then, our eyes nomadic,
knowing we knew about things too sacred to say.

Alaska, I was there—

visiting a school and Tommy was the boy
who loved poetry and this was

Tommy's father. He had his own poetry in him
or perhaps his life was a poem, in the lyrical strides he took

through the wilderness, or the epic tale
of his time on Saint Lawrence Island

when he harpooned with the Yupik tribe, out at sea whaling
in the original way, the way

of connecting first with the mind of the whale
that presents itself, sacrificially.

Eye of the whale and the eye of man,
a certain reverence occurs

just like Tommy's father and me
how our souls peered out from our bodies

and we knew we were shades of each other, wanderers
of different lands but carrying the same furtive beliefs.

Of the whale, the whale too, was a poem—

when it danced before the old boat
how willingly it dipped and surfaced and blew

before arrows pierced the long, holy length of its body
and still it gave of itself

calmly above water it stayed
and it stayed held

by the bladder bags of seals, puffed with air,
to keep it afloat.

And this a poem, in the way the whale was buoyant for days
blood-letting, like the very words which surface

from within the salty sea of our bodies,
thoughts that slowly drain from us

before we tow them in, before we write them out,
blessing our beasts as they come ashore.

The Death of Your Body

I wonder how it will happen, Father,
when you, in your bed, are leaving yourself,
rising out of the lame structure you inhabited,
that moments before was shrinking
another inch down in a chair
giving off sighs against gravity
for your limbs falling backwards....
Will your eyes that stopped seeing me
suddenly close?
When I think of your moment of death
I want life as an eternal form brightening
the room where we bend over your body.
I think of words never said
coming to me as light.
I see myself simply glowing with your sentences,
nothing dramatic or as pathetic
as the one child you bore
who would not eat for a year
after your brain damage, was starved
for your love.

Turns

I can no longer stand
how you are something alive,
but not quite living

a figure
cast down
as a shadow

turning old,
at your great age
into a child again.

Look at me.

At least offer
that blind stare
for I have come
out of love
and will leave crying
in the stairwell,
and then drive away
damaged.

Listen.

How hard
this continues to be
more than your suffering

even the spinning clock
wants to end
these hours
of shallow breathing.

Hear what else
pivots away.

The cold meals,
the nurse that tires of
rotating your body.

Mother,

I read the lines of your palm
as long roads of endurance, miles of sacrifice
that led to this hospital bed, where you parked
beside my dying father and took his hand in yours
and did not move.

I felt changed by the gesture, stunned
that the quiet work of a hand could do so much,
such a small act, one hand cupping another's—
it had me retreating into a corner
made of curtains, white and loosely draped
as angel wings.

There is no way to say it. There is something
to be said. Perhaps distance brought me close
to understanding—

what endurance was, but also unwavering love
so that all our years caretaking ceased in that moment,
and the scene became a privilege
to watch....

And then your hand simply returned to being
a hand, every finger of kindness
like any other object of light

like a pearl perhaps, hidden inside the dark,
oppressive shell of an oyster—
something that would glow no matter what:
into the night, into my father's last days
and nights, to the very end.

The Bottom Stones

The Natives say that stones hold the history of a place,
they say you can hold a stone in your hand
and discern its mystery

that your palm will read it,
that your palm too can be read, like rivulets
its lines go outward in meaningful phrases, like tributaries
they drain into the knowing sea of your hand.

If all can be known by touch all has a message
even the tiniest pebble, even today
standing beside an untamed brook
as I peer through its clear look down to
its gravel bed

I understand how the current takes to it things
like my own path on land
and its sudden events

I notice the bottom stones
who hear laps of water and remember them right,
are constantly talked to by current.

Today, while the brook announces itself, my hand
skims its surface before sinking
down to these small bodies of rock, back
to the clarity our fingers first had
before time.

Making a Path Called *Charles*

Nearing death was light,
nearing light a long way back
to remembering, with nothing before me
but floating rubble, pieces of truth
to trip over and I was to form
from this, a road.

I was to match scenes,
piecing together the light and dark
colors of incidents,
like a puzzle to solve that
I had not wanted, but it was a way
you see, for there was nothing to walk on,
nowhere to go, not anything else but
an awful quiet.

And I was to stand
on each stone in place

stay, at times, for what seemed like days
learning the life I had lived
while the stones told words to my feet
and they entered my body.

There were formidable piles
that held my own history, spreading
for miles with sounds coming forth
that was my dementia, and still my task was
to take up these rocks,
shaking them alive.

I was to learn my wife's courage
where joy barely entered.

I was to shape what stones knew
of deranged hours, and trail across this

strange world that occurred, only stopping
before that final wreckage,
my daughter's, the untold ruins

of her and me, the rocks that say
it is not possible to remain before them,
and not be destroyed.

Aerial View

In your world
it was winter. It was cold.

The clouds opened
as night came
and from them
the selfless falling
of angelical snow

a crumbling heaven
then silence, the earth so
white-laden.

What peace it would teach
the dark

how you would feel
me easing
into a clarity
I had not known
in thirty years

a realm
of being once more
of sound mind
out of my ill body
long before the last breath.

     *

Daughter, you sat
through timed moments.

I flew alert
toward weatherless light

you paced through that
vacant look of the streets, going
going under
the giant holiness of trees
but never once
saying aloud
what you thought of
never out loud
even days after

my flesh took to cold
soil, could you admit
your thinking
to anyone.
Say it now though
just once

how you have felt
your mind break
because of me.

*

Dementia
that word, what it is made of

speak it where
no one will know

softly to plants
you love so deep
in safe woods

like telling on a bad dream,
that it would be gone.

Admit my life destroyed yours
and hear then how
air answers

for there will be
such moving language, a forgiving
breeze which knows
my behaviors
were not of
choice.

My grown little girl,
go where the wind talks
as it covers you saying

what I only wanted
to be
your good father.

Reading the Thoughts of Clouds

The clouds do not speak to us as clouds
they talk of things other than weather,
at times they appear like a train's readable smoke
or as a plane's contrail scribbling a message
against the blue notion of sky

today, while hiking, they stretch for miles
in a language of wisp-like strands, as a long running sentence
through mountains and we stand, we look up, saying
if we just stay long enough we'll know
what they have given the sky,
they have given ourselves.

To know ourselves, we say,
is to also know these streaks which turn fingerlike
pointing things out to us, what they mean when they come
with storms or sun shining through.

Certain Shadows Over the Mountain

There is magic in this story,
in shadow-play, in the way a hiker stood on a cliff

with his face upturned, his mouth slightly open.
Maybe he was grieving. This, I do not know.

Maybe the hiker needed an answer to a question
for which he held no words

and so a thought rose instinctively, its voice
silently lifted as does helium in balloons.

You must know a second mountain loomed across from him.
You must also know the day was windless

yet when his thoughts reached the blue tip of the sky
a cloud began traveling in front of the sun

it moved slow while he remained on the ridge,
his eyes fixed on nothing but what he was thinking.

You must know that another cloud began
crossing another cloud until the sun

spread shadows long over the second mountain's
green blur of trees and the dark

silhouettes roamed openly as animals
in shapes designed to teach him things,

like bones or tea leaves they fell as answers
only he could know. He could feel his own story too,

shifting, becoming clear in himself and his eyes, they
were not cool stones anymore, behind them was knowledge

to leave the slippery cliff,
his legs in a language so very exact walking

like shadows over the uncertain earth, noting the ease,
the sureness of his steps if he would let them. If he would allow

each foot continuing where it needed to, going
wherever it should go from there.

The Cleansing

When my body was ready I went with my body
though the wind hit, hurting my face.

Behind two women I walked, going
where they went up the snowy incline of a mountain

wearing boots and a bathrobe, continuing
from the cabin to the wooden hut, built years ago.

It was dark inside but for a wood stove,
the orange of its fire

and someone mentioned the heat in that moment
but really the moment was about the way

our robes fell from us, how we stood
before a bowl of dry rocks near to the flame of the stove;

it was about the stones on the stove
and the stove and the flames of it and our bodies.

It was misty in there and there were platforms
with bowls of cool water

and we sat among them and among them
were lit candles

and on the platforms were vials
of scented oils and porous rocks and cloths.

It was quiet before someone mentioned
Alaska, its winters, the cold

of it, of the air and its untamed breath;
then another spoke of the sky

how night appears in layers of deepening color
that each minute holds

a smoky blueness
which darkens before the black comes in.

Of the blackness I learned how it ribbons
the mountain down to the river

of the river I heard how it carries within,
such ancient tales.

I wanted to speak but needed more than words.
I wanted words but the ones I thought of

held no images, to cleanse the rivers
in me: storied rivers, the hidden

waters, nameless.

When Just Enough Words . . .

have gathered at windows,

while I speak   only
as loud as
weariness allows

after all
has been said
repeated to
only myself   alone
in a room

when just enough words   when the glass fogs

and the world outside is
blotted out—

I want to break through
become

my own human story, the one I keep
inside myself.

What I am saying is   what I am speaking of
is hard to state

the words that come seem awkward
and hurried and

never fully divulge
what trails us, this illness
my mother now has.

Go on, I tell myself. Just say the word *dementia*

watch it stick to the pane
see it
spread
once more
onto the glass
suddenly

Notes

"Phrases Strong and Perfect" references Linky, an Eskimo elder of the Inupiaq tribe on White Mountain, Alaska, where I had the privilege of learning from the elders.

The inspiration for "Clan of the Owl" comes from Rose, an elder on White Mountain, who is Linky's sister. These sisters belong to the Owl Clan of the White Mountain tribe. The story relayed in the poem is a true occurrence involving Rose's great-uncle Percy (also referred to as Grandpa in Eskimo tradition) and the drowning of his son, Alan. Tribal stories are sacred, and so it is with appreciation to be given Rose's story, to commit to written words.

"After Alaska" and "Making of the Eskimo Clothes" respond to and incorporate the life of Lisa, a librarian in Homer, Alaska, who is Caucasian and married an Inupiaq man, and then spent over a decade in the far north, immersed in true Eskimo culture and subsistence living.

"The Yukon Quest" is inspired by the true story of Greg Parvin. The Yukon Quest is a dog-sled race that mushers and their dog teams must complete before racing in the Iditarod. Although this race does not receive as much notoriety as the Iditarod, it has proven to be more difficult.

In Gratitude

I want to acknowledge the Alaskan Arts Council for teaching-artist residencies that inspired many poems; as well as Acadia National Park, Virginia Center for the Creative Arts and Vermont Studio Center, for residencies that gave me time to write. I am very grateful to NJ State Council on the Arts for a Poetry Fellowship; and the Geraldine R. Dodge Foundation for a Fellowship to Vermont Studio Center.

And last, my ongoing thanks to those who provided house-sitting opportunities while I wrote this book, and to my editor Tom Lombardo, for his keen eye and encouragement. A very special thanks to Barbara and David Daniels, to Paul Lisicky, Joe Barbarese, Elaine Terranova and Mike Northen who responded to these poems along the way; and to Pam Interlante, loyal friend and supporter of my life on the road.

T.H.

THÉRÈSE HALSCHEID's previous poetry collections include *Powertalk, Without Home, Uncommon Geography*, which won a finalist award for the Paterson Poetry Book Prize; and *Greatest Hits*, a chapbook award from *Pudding House Publications*.

She received her MA from Rowan and MFA from Rutgers University, and currently teaches for Atlantic Cape Community College, New Jersey. Through cultural exchange programs she has traveled widely, and taught in England and Russia. Through the Alaskan Arts Council, she had the privilege of working with an Inupiaq Eskimo tribe on White Mountain, as well as a residency in Homer.

For the past two decades, the author has been house-sitting—caring for others' homes and animals—while writing. This mobility, along with simple living, has helped her to sustain her writing life. Her photography chronicles her journey, and has been in juried shows.

Learn more about Thérèse at www.ThereseHalscheid.com.

COVER ARTIST DAVID HAYWARD runs a blog called nakedpastor where he displays his cartoons, art, and writing. He also moderates an online community called The Lasting Supper that provides resources for people desiring spiritual independence. David and his wife Lisa live on the east coast of Canada.

CPSIA information can be obtained at www.ICGtesting.com
Printed in the USA
BVOW07s1046031114

373436BV00003B/225/P